The GROSS AND GOOFY Body

Give Me a Hand

The Secrets of Hands, Feet, Arms, and Legs

By Melissa Stewart

Illustrated by Janet Hamlin

mc Marshall Cavendish
Benchmark
New York

THIS BOOK WAS MADE POSSIBLE, IN PART, BY A GRANT FROM THE SOCIETY OF CHILDREN'S BOOK WRITERS AND ILLUSTRATORS.

Published by Marshall Cavendish Benchmark
An imprint of Marshall Cavendish Corporation

Other Marshall Cavendish Offices:
Marshall Cavendish International (Asia) Private Limited, 1 New Industrial Road, Singapore 536196 • Marshall Cavendish International (Thailand) Co Ltd. 253 Asoke, 12th Flr, Sukhumvit 21 Road, Klongtoey Nua, Wattana, Bangkok 10110, Thailand • Marshall Cavendish (Malaysia) Sdn Bhd, Times Subang, Lot 46,
Subang Hi-Tech Industrial Park, Batu Tiga, 40000 Shah Alam, Selangor Darul Ehsan, Malaysia

Marshall Cavendish is a trademark of Times Publishing Limited

All websites were available and accurate when this book was sent to press.

Library of Congress Cataloging-in-Publication Data
Stewart, Melissa.
Give me a hand : the secrets of hands, feet, arms, and legs / by Melissa Stewart.
p. cm. — (The gross and goofy body)
Summary: "Provides comprehensive information on the role hands, feet, arms, and legs play in the body science of humans and animals"--Provided by the publisher.
Includes index.
ISBN 978-0-7614-4158-8
1. Hand — Juvenile literature. 2. Foot — Juvenile literature. 3. Extremities (Anatomy) — Juvenile literature. 4. Body, Human — Juvenile literature. I. Title.
QL950.7.S74 2010
591.4—dc22
2008033618

Editor: Joy Bean
Publisher: Michelle Bisson
Art Director: Anahid Hamparian
Series Designer: Daniel Roode

Photo research by Tracey Engel
Cover photo: Getty Images/Westend61

The photographs in this book are used by permission and through the courtesy of: Alamy: Woodbridge Wildlife Images, 27 (top). CORBIS: Michael & Patricia Fogden, 5 (right). Getty Images: Iconica/Commercial Eye, 4; Gallo Images/Shem Compion, 5 (left); Photographer's Choice/Kaz Chiba, 6; The Image Bank/Andy Caulfield, 7; Iconica/ Robert Manella, 8 (left); Absodels, 8 (right); Taxi/Nick Dolding, 9; The Image Bank/ Jose Luis Pelaez, 10; Iconica/Philip and Karen Smith, 12; Taxi/David McGlynn, 13; Photodisc/Thomas Northcut, 14; Photonica/Michael Hall, 16; Photographer's Choice/Steven Hunt, 21 (bottom); Taxi/Gail Shumway, 21 (top); The Image Bank/Andy Rouse, 24; Dorling Kindersley/Frank Greenaway, 26, 27 (bottom), 34 (right); Riser/Simon Wilkinson, 34 (left); Dorling Kindersley/Jane Burton, 35; Visuals Unlimited/Robert & Jean Pollock, 36 (left); Photolibrary/Emanuele Biggi, 36 (right); Dorling Kindersley/John Daniels, 37 (left); National Geographic/Timothy Laman, 37 (right); Dorling Kindersley/Russell Sadur, 38; Dorling Kindersley/Dave King, 39. Photo Researchers, Inc.: Friedrich Saurer, 17 (top); Biophoto Associates, 17 (bottom); Andrew Syred, 29 (top); W. Treat Davidson, 29 (bottom).

Printed in Malaysia (T)
135642

CONTENTS

ARMED AND READY!

You're trying to do your homework. But all you can think about are the chocolate-chip cookies cooling on the kitchen counter.

You aren't supposed to have any until after dinner. But your stomach's rumbling, and you just can't wait. You hop to your feet and run downstairs.

Your legs sprint across the living room and dart into the kitchen. The coast is clear, so you lift your arm, stretch out your hand, and grab a cookie. Then you pop it in your mouth. Mmmm! Delicious!

You could survive without hands, arms, legs, and feet, but you wouldn't have as much fun. You couldn't sneak a cookie or kick a soccer ball. You couldn't chase after your sister or give her a noogie. And how on Earth would you scratch your itchy nose? You'll be amazed at all the ways hands, arms, legs, and feet make life better for you—and for other animals, too.

Why can a jacana walk on floating plants? Because its long, thin toes spread out the bird's body weight.

A sloth uses its superstrong arm and leg muscles to dangle from tree branches. As long as the shaggy-coated creature stays silent and still, it's hard to spot.

GIVE ME A HAND!

You're lucky to have hands. You use them to write and to draw and to button your shirt. They're also perfect for climbing a wall, catching a ball, or squirting your little brother with the garden hose.

A dog's paws can't do any of these things. Neither can a horse's hooves, a bat's wings, or a seal's flippers.

What makes a hand so, uhh, handy? It's not the broad palm or the four long fingers. Believe it or not, it's the short, stumpy thumb.

A thumb is **opposable**. That means it's set opposite your fingers, and it can swivel to touch them. Your thumb lets you use your hand in all kinds of ways.

Thumbs Up !

People aren't the only animals with opposable thumbs. Chimps, bonobos, gorillas, and orangutans have them, too. They're our closest relatives in the animal world.

Most of the monkeys in Africa and Asia have opposable thumbs and big toes. Monkeys in Central and South America have only opposable big toes, so their hands can't grip, grab, or grasp like yours.

GET A GRIP!

Thanks to your talented thumb and its four nifty neighbors, you can grip and hold things in three different ways.

Hook Grip

When you open a door, you hook your fingers around the knob and pull it toward you. You use the same kind of grip to lift a drinking glass or a book.

Power Grip

To hold a knife, you rest the handle in the palm of your hand and wrap your fingers around it. You use the same kind of grip to hold a toothbrush.

Precision Grip

When you pick up a small object, such as a coin or a peanut, you hold it between the tips of your thumb and index finger.

A Curious Collection

Some people collect stamps or baseball cards, but not Adrian Flatt. The retired hand surgeon has been making bronze casts of people's hands for more than forty years. His collection includes samples from dozens of doctors, eight presidents, and twelve astronauts. But he didn't stop there. He also has hand casts of Walt Disney, the actor Paul Newman, the artist Norman Rockwell, the magician David Copperfield, and the wrestler Andre the Giant.

YOU'VE GOT NERVE!

As your hands push, pull, pinch, and poke, nearly 35,000 sensors in your skin collect information about the outside world. Each one is at the tip of a long, stringy nerve that carries messages to your brain.

Want to find them? Here's how. Draw a postage stamp-sized box on the back of your hand. Divide it into sixteen smaller squares by drawing three lines across and three lines up and down. Now draw a larger version of the box on a piece of paper.

Pressure Sensors

Straighten out a paper clip, and use the tip to touch each square on the back of your hand. If you feel it pressing against your skin, write a P in the same square on the piece of paper.

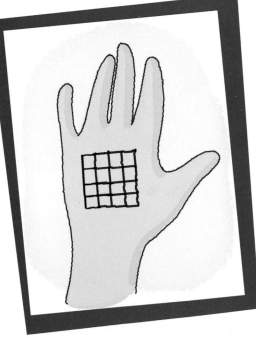

Cold Sensors

Hold the tip of the paper clip against an ice cube. Then use it to touch one of the squares on your hand. If you feel it, write a *C* in the same square on the piece of paper. Cool the paper clip again before testing the next square.

Heat Sensors

Dip the tip of the paper clip into warm water and count to ten. Now touch one of the squares on your hand. Can you feel it? If you can, write an *H* in the same square on the piece of paper. Be sure to reheat the paper clip between each test.

Pain Sensors

Hmm, do you really want to poke around for pain sensors? Let's just say we know they're there.

When you've finished your tests, look at the piece of paper. Are you surprised by the results?

FANTASTIC FINGERS

Peas.
Pins.
Pebbles.
Pennies.

You couldn't pick up these itty-bitty items if you couldn't feel them. Luckily, your fingers are the most sensitive part of your body.

But to grasp small objects, you need more than sensitive skin. You need traction action, and that's where the ridges on your fingertips come in handy. Believe it or not, they do more than leave greasy fingerprints on the fridge. Like the treads on a tire, finger ridges grab a surface and prevent slipping and skidding.

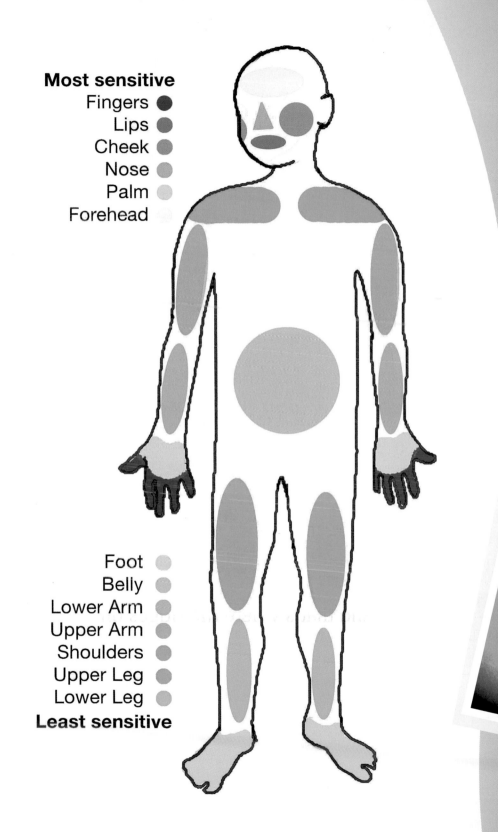

Most sensitive
Fingers ●
Lips ●
Cheek ●
Nose ●
Palm ●
Forehead

Foot ●
Belly ●
Lower Arm ●
Upper Arm ●
Shoulders ●
Upper Leg ●
Lower Leg ●
Least sensitive

Prints and Patterns

The ridges on your fingertips are arranged in patterns made up of loops, whorls, and arches. When you touch something, you leave behind fingerprints with your unique pattern.

UNDER YOUR SKIN

To really understand how hands work, you'd have to peel back your skin and take a closer look.

Don't want to make a bloody mess? No problem. Just look at the diagrams on page 15. What you'll see are twenty-seven bones and more than thirty muscles. The bones give your hand its shape and strength. The muscles control every move your hand makes.

Five long, thin bones called **metacarpals** span your palm.

Each finger has three **phalanges**. Your thumb has two.

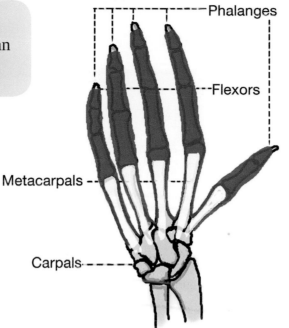

Phalanges

Flexors

Metacarpals

Carpals

The eight small, cube-shaped **carpal** bones in your wrist are arranged in two rows of four. They let you bend and twist your hand in any direction.

Flexor muscles bend your fingers and thumb. They're located on the back of your forearm. Bands of tissue called **tendons** attach them to your phalanges.

The midpalmar muscles bend and straighten the **joints** between your phalanges and metacarpals.

The thenar muscles let your thumb grasp objects.

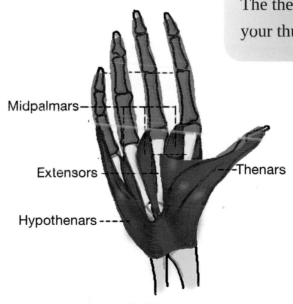

Midpalmars

Extensors

Hypothenars

Thenars

The extensor muscles straighten your fingers and thumb. They're located on the back of your forearm, and tendons attach them to your phalanges.

The hypothenar muscles let you stick your little finger straight out while making a fist. It's almost impossible to do this with your ring finger.

HOW ABOUT A KNUCKLE SANDWICH?

Just kidding! Nobody wants to be punched in the mouth!

A **knuckle** is a joint—the area where two bones meet. It's where your fingers bend when you make a fist.

You have knuckles between your phalanges and between your phalanges and metacarpals. A liquid called **synovial fluid** fills the space between the bones.

Some people like to "crack" their knuckles. Are you one of them? When you pull on a knuckle, the pressure inside it drops. Your **ligaments**—the bands of tissue that stretch across joints—get sucked in, and tiny

Take a close look at this diagram of the hand. The muscles are shown in red. Tendons and ligaments are colored white. You can even see bones in some spots.

bubbles form in your synovial fluid.

No one knows what causes the spine-chilling sound you hear when you crack your knuckles. It might be ligaments snapping back into place. Or maybe it's vibrations caused by bubbles bursting inside your synovial fluid. Either way, you shouldn't crack your knuckles too often. It can weaken your hands.

Bizarre Bending

Can you bend your fingers back toward your wrist? People might say you're double-jointed, but that's not really true. It just means your joints are extra flexible. Maybe the ends of your bones are smoother than normal, or perhaps your ligaments are extra stretchy.

YOUR HANDS SAY SO

When you and a friend are spying on your sister, you need to communicate without saying a word. What do you do? You use your hands.

When your friend needs to be quiet, you hold a finger in front of your mouth. When you want him to follow you, you wave your fingers toward you. You hold up your hand when you want him to stop. And when everything's okay, you give your friend a thumbs-up. How many other hand signals can you think of?

When you talk to people, it's a good idea to keep an eye on their hands. When people keep their hands open, with the palms up, they feel friendly and are probably telling the truth. If people hide their hands or have their palms down, they could be lying. Or they might be feeling angry or worried. And if you see a clenched fist . . . RUN!

Helping Hands

Long ago, many different American Indian groups lived on the Great Plains of North America. Each group spoke a slightly different language. When people from different groups met, they sometimes used a common sign language to communicate.

WHAT'S IN A NAME?

Arms. They're those long, strong limbs sticking out of your shoulders. They bend at the elbows, so you can swat a fly. And they twist at your wrist, so you can write and draw.

You need arms to lift your backpack and to stuff food into your mouth. And they're a big help when you want to bat a ball or stash secret stuff on the top shelf of your closet. It's hard to imagine life without arms.

We usually think of arms as **limbs** that grab, reach, or lift, while legs are limbs that walk, jump, and run. But with some animals, it's hard to tell the difference.

Lobsters, crabs, and scorpions fight off enemies and grab prey with clawlike pincers on their front limbs. Are those limbs arms or legs? It depends on who you ask.

A praying mantis has six legs, but it walks on only four. It uses its front legs to catch prey.

A sea star's feet are on the underside of its arms.

An octopus uses its arms to grab **prey** and to jet through the water.

OPEN ARMED

Your arms can push, pull, and pivot. They lift and bend, too. With so many movements, you might think your arms are just as complex as your hands. But think again! Each arm contains just three bones. They work with nearby muscles to do their duty every day.

Bones

Humerus

Radius

Ulna

Your **humerus** bone is inside your upper arm. It extends from your shoulder to your elbow.

Your **radius** bone runs from your elbow to your wrist—on the same side of your arm as your thumb. You can rotate your radius around your ulna to hold your hand palm up or palm down.

Your **ulna** bone runs from your elbow to your wrist. It's on the same side of your arm as your little finger.

Your deltoid muscle wraps around your shoulder. You use it when you hold your arm out straight or lift it above your head.

Muscles

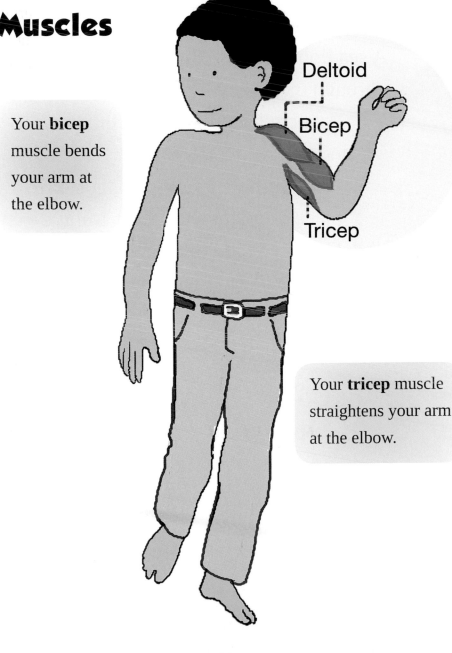

Deltoid

Bicep

Tricep

Your **bicep** muscle bends your arm at the elbow.

Your **tricep** muscle straightens your arm at the elbow.

Tugging Teams

Many muscles work together to help you move. Your biceps and triceps are a perfect example. Try bending your arm at the elbow. Now straighten it. First, your bicep pulls your lower arm up. Then, your tricep pulls your lower arm back down. The muscles are like two groups of people battling it out in a tug-of-war match.

DARE TO COMPARE

A bat's wide wings soar through the sky. A sea lion's flexible flippers cruise through the sea.

A horse's long, graceful limbs race across grassy plains.

Mammals live in all kinds of places, and they use their front limbs in many different ways. But sneak a peek at what's underneath it all, and you might be surprised.

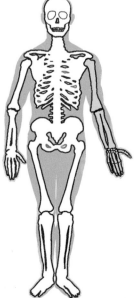

A human has long arms that bend at the elbow and hands with opposable thumbs.

24

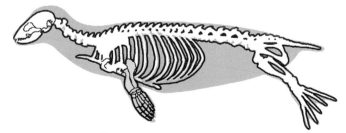

A bat's arm bones look a lot like yours, but its hand bones sure don't. Its long, lean metacarpals and phalanges support the thin skin that stretches over them.

Below a horse's hoof is the same bone as is found in your fingertip. The horse's long phalanges and metacarpals form its lower limb, while its short ulna, radius, and humerus form its upper limb.

A seal's short, thick arm bones provide the power that propels it through the water. Its tiny hand bones make its flipper more flexible.

Ancient Arms

Most dinosaurs walked on four legs, but not *T. rex*. It had two tiny arms with sharp claws. How did the massive meat eater use its little limbs? Nobody knows. They were strong enough to hold prey but too short to reach *T. rex's* mouth.

MOVIN' AND GROOVIN'

Scoot. Skip. Scramble.
Run. Race. Ramble.
Dodge. Dart. Dance.
Pace. Plod. Prance.

Who would have
guessed that there are so
many ways to move from place
to place? But you couldn't do any
of them without legs. Your legs support your
body and take you everywhere you want to go.
You have two legs. So do birds and bats and
some salamanders. But most animals have many more.

Cats, dogs, crocodiles, and frogs are just a few examples of four-legged animals. Insects have six legs, and spiders have eight. Crabs and shrimp have ten legs, while pill bugs have fourteen.

Most centipedes have around fifty legs, but some have more than two hundred. Millipedes, like the one below, have the most legs of all—up to four hundred. Just imagine what they'd look like doing a jig!

Evolution in Action

Brown anoles usually live on the ground. Long, strong legs help the little lizards chase down crickets, roaches, and other tasty treats.

Curly-tailed lizards are bigger, faster, and tougher. When these hungry hunters invaded the Brown anole's habitat, the little lizards took to the trees. In just a year the anole population had shorter, stockier legs to help them scamper along branches and clamber up trunks.

MORE THAN MOVING

There's no doubt that legs are a great way to get around. But you use them in other ways, too. They're perfect for kneeing a soccer ball or shutting a door when your hands are full. And when you sit down, a cute kitty can curl up in your lap.

People aren't the only ones who use their legs in all kinds of ways. Other animals do, too.

A male platypus stabs its enemies with sharp, poisonous spurs on the backs of its legs.

Dragonfly **larvae** bend their legs to create a net that's perfect for catching mosquitoes, gnats, and other tasty treats.

Crickets and katydids listen for mating calls with the ears on their knees.

A female tachinid fly's ears are near the tops of her legs. She uses them to locate other insects so she can spray them with larvae. The young flies burrow into unsuspecting insects and devour them from the inside out. Yuck!

As a daddy longlegs races across the ground, it waves its two longest legs in the air. They help the daddy longlegs hear, smell, and taste.

As a honeybee collects **pollen** from flowers, it stores the nutritious food in tiny baskets on its back legs.

A LOOK INSIDE LEGS

Bones

It's no wonder that we sometimes have trouble telling the difference between arms and legs. Inside and out, they have a lot in common. To see this for yourself, compare the diagrams shown here to the ones on pages 22 and 23.

The femur is your body's longest, strongest bone. Sometimes called the thigh bone, it runs from your hip to your knee.

The patella, a thick, triangular bone, is sometimes called the kneecap. It covers and protects your knee.

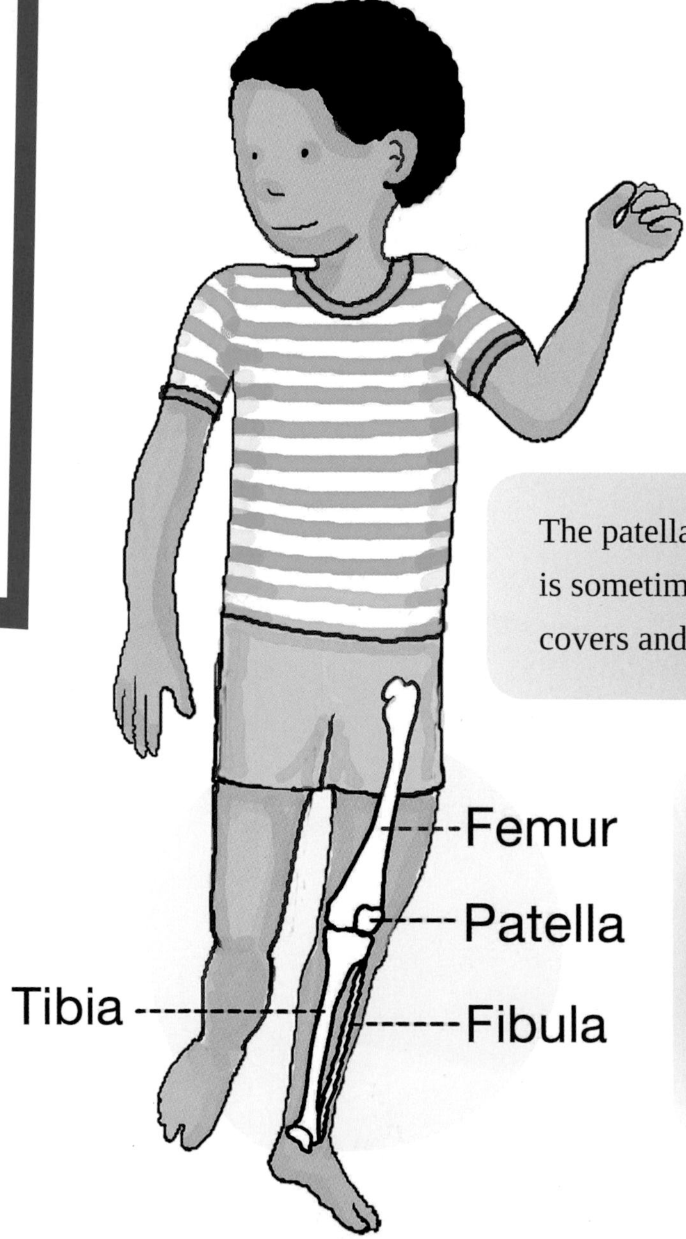

The fibula bone is located on the outside of your lower leg and is much thinner than your tibia. It helps control ankle movements.

Located on the inside of your lower leg, the **tibia** bone runs from your knee to your ankle and supports your body's weight.

Femur

Patella

Tibia

Fibula

Muscles

The vastus muscles straighten your knee. They're important for walking, running, jumping, and squatting.

The sartorius is a long, thin muscle runs down the length of your thigh. It bends and rotates your knee and hip.

The shin muscle lifts your foot and stabilizes your ankle while you walk. It also locks your ankle when you kick something with your toes.

The calf muscles bend your foot up and down. When you jump, they act like shock absorbers.

Sartorius

Vastus muscles

Calf muscle

Shin muscle

FACTS ABOUT FEET

Now that you've seen how much legs and arms have in common, it shouldn't surprise you that feet and hands are similar too.

But while hands are tools for grasping and grabbing, feet are platforms. Your tarsals and metatarsals are arched to spread out your body's weight. Your short, fat toes help you balance when you stand.

Tendons attach the flexor muscles to your phalanges and let you bend your toes.

Flexors

Metatarsals

Phalanges

Tarsals

The **tarsals** are seven bones that form your ankle and the back of your foot. They support most of your body's weight.

Your big toe has two phalanges. The rest of your toes have three.

The **metatarsals** are five long, thin bones that span the arch of your foot.

The extensor muscles straighten your toes. Like **flexors**, they're located on top of your **tarsals**, and tendons attach them to your phalanges.

Peroneuses

Extensors

Adductors

The peroneus muscles bend your foot at the ankle.

Abductors

The abductor muscles stretch your big and little toes out to the sides.

The adductor muscles pull your big and little toes closer to your other toes.

Needle-y Nerves

When bundles of **nerves** in your foot get smooshed, they can "fall asleep." What should you do? Don't let your sleeping dogs lie. As soon as you stand up and walk around, the tingly feeling will go away.

WAYS OF WALKING

Whether you stroll, strut, or stomp, you take about eight thousand steps every day. And you keep on going day after day, month after month, year after year.

Believe it or not, you'll walk about 115,000 miles (185,075 kilometers) in your life. If all that trekking and trudging were in a straight line, you could circle the equator four and a half times!

When you walk, you place the full length of your foot on the ground during each stride. So do bears, baboons, rabbits, and raccoons.

Most meat-eating mammals walk on their toes, with the back part of the foot raised. To see what this looks like, watch a cat or dog as it runs through your yard.

Horses and deer walk on their tippy toes. Because these animals can really reach out during each **stride**, they move very fast.

No Cheese, Please !

As you peel off your sock, you notice a strange smell and look at your foot. There's the culprit—white globs of caking, crumbling gunk. Yup, you guessed it—toe cheese.

Toe cheese is a mangled mash of dead skin cells, dirt, **bacteria**, and sock lint. It builds up between your toes when you don't wash your feet often enough. Yuck!

FANCY FEET

Want to know where an animal lives and how it survives? Just look at its feet.

Some feet flee fast, while others leap out of harm's way. Some feet swim to safety, while others scramble up steep cliffs. Animal feet can also dig, glide, stick, and slide. They're the perfect tools for finding food and avoiding enemies.

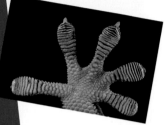

The sticky pads on a gecko's toes help it dart up tree trunks and scamper along branches.

A turkey uses its large toes and sharp toenails to scratch the ground in search of insects and other tasty treats.

When a snail is on the move, it lays down a trail of slippery slime and slides across it with its muscular foot.

Want to see how your body measures up? Try this.

Grab a ruler and measure your thumb. Is it 1 inch (2.5 centimeters) across?

Measure your foot. Is it 1 foot (30 cm) long?

Try measuring your parents' thumbs and feet. Are they the "right" size?

Ask you parents to use their car's odometer to measure out 1 mile (1.6 km). Count your steps as you walk the distance. Does it take one thousand double paces to go the distance? Why do you think people used to rely on body parts to measure distances?

From measuring distances and dancing a jig to throwing a ball and picking up pennies, it's hard to believe all the ways feet, legs, arms, and hands help us every day. And we aren't alone. Many other animals depend on them, too.

GLOSSARY

bacterium (pl. bacteria)—A tiny, one-celled living thing that reproduces by dividing. Some bacteria can make people sick.

bicep— The muscle that bends the arm at the elbow. A bicep and tricep work as a team. When one contracts, the other relaxes.

carpal—One of the bones that supports the wrist.

flexor—A muscle that bends a finger or toe. Its partner is an extensor, which straightens the same finger or toe.

humerus—The bone that runs between the shoulder and the elbow.

joint—The place where two bones meet.

knuckle—A joint in the hand or foot. In your hand, it's the place where your fingers bend when you make a fist.

larva (pl. larvae)—The second stage in the life cycle of many insects.

ligament—A band of tissue that stretches across a joint.

limb—A branch or offshoot. Your arms and legs branch off the trunk, or main part, of your body.

mammal—A warm-blooded animal that has a backbone and feeds its young mother's milk. Almost all mammals have some hair or fur.

metacarpal—A bone that supports the palm of the hand.

metatarsal— A bone that supports the center of the foot.

nerve—A cell that carries messages to and from the brain.

opposable—Capable of being placed opposite something else. An opposable thumb is set opposite the four fingers, making it easier to grasp and hold objects.

phalange—One of the bones that support fingers and toes.

pollen—A powdery material released from plants. It floats in the air and can irritate the nose.

prey—An animal that is hunted by a predator.

radius—The bone that runs from your elbow to your wrist.

stride—When an animal is walking or running, the series of foot and leg movements that occur between times when all feet are on the ground.

synovial fluid—The fluid inside a joint.

tarsal—One of the bones found at the rear of the foot.

tendon—A band of strong, stretchy tissue that joins muscles to bones.

tibia—A thick, strong bone that runs from the knee to the ankle. It supports the body's weight.

tricep—The muscle that straightens the arm at the elbow. A bicep and tricep work as a team. When one contracts, the other relaxes.

ulna—A bone that runs from the elbow to the wrist.

A NOTE ON SOURCES

Dear Readers,

Give Me a Hand! is full of fascinating facts that come from all kinds of sources. Most of the information about muscles, bones, and nerves comes from medical textbooks that focus on anatomy and physiology. The rest comes from high school science textbooks and articles from popular science magazines.

This book includes some great information about how animals use their limbs. I found it by looking through dozens of books about animals and animal behavior.

I also searched for interesting information on the Internet. That's how I learned about the role body parts played in ancient measuring systems and that American Indians sometimes used sign language to communicate.

Finally, I checked some of my research with doctors and scientists to make sure I had the most up-to-date information. Those interviews helped me understand the debate about how *T. rex* used its arms. And they even provided some great new information, including that dogs and cats can be left-handed or right-handed.

—Melissa Stewart

FIND OUT MORE

BOOKS

Amazing Animals of the World. New York: Scholastic Library, 2006.

Green, Jen. *Muscles.* Corona, CA: Stargazer Books, 2006.

Green, Jen. *Skeleton.* Corona, CA: Stargazer Books, 2006.

Stewart, Melissa. *Extreme Nature.* New York: HarperCollins, 2006.

Stewart, Melissa. *Use Your Senses!* Minneapolis, MN: Compass Point Books, 2005.

WEBSITES

Guinness World Records
This site contains up-to-date information on some of the strangest world records you can imagine.
http://www.guinnessworldrecords.com/default.aspx

Kids Health
This site answers just about any question you might have about your body and keeping it healthy.
http://kidshealth.org/kid

That Explains It!
All kinds of interesting information about the human body, animals, food, inventions and machines, and more can be found at this site.
http://www.coolquiz.com/trivia/explain

INDEX

Page numbers in **bold** are illustrations.

ABOUT THE AUTHOR

Melissa Stewart has written everything from board books for preschoolers to magazine articles for adults. She is the award-winning author of more than one hundred books for young readers. She serves on the board of advisors of the Society of Children's Book Writers and Illustrators and is a judge for the American Institute of Physics Children's Science Writing Award. Stewart earned a B.S. in biology from Union College and an M.A. in science journalism from New York University. She lives in Acton, Massachusetts, with her husband, Gerard. To learn more about Stewart, please visit her website: www.melissa-stewart.com.

ABOUT THE ILLUSTRATOR

Janet Hamlin has illustrated many children's books, games, newspapers, and even Harry Potter stuff. She is also a court artist. The Gross and Goofy Body is one of her all-time favorite series, and she now considers herself the factoid queen of bodily functions. She lives and draws in New York and loves it.